SUDDENLY
IN
CHARGE

One woman's journey navigating unanticipated fears and anxieties in a male-dominated workforce

MORGAN WRAY

© 2023 by Morgan Wray.
All rights reserved. No portion of this book may be reproduced, stored in a retrieval system, or transmitted in any form or by any means - electronic, mechanical, photocopy, recording, scanning, or other - except for brief quotations in critical reviews or articles, without the prior written permission of the author.

INTRODUCTION

Being in the middle of a storm of change in life can be a terrifying experience. Panic, anxiety, and confusion swirl all around. The noise they make can thunder so loudly in your ears that you are incapable of hearing yourself think. Negative thoughts tend to creep into your head and heart to the point that breathing becomes a strenuous task. But the most frightening part of it all, more than the noise or the choking fear, is the absence of hope. On the darkest days, amid the transitions in our lives, the flame of hope threatens to burn out. Seemingly out of nowhere you find yourself asking, "How can I go on? What hope is there for me to succeed?"

This is my story of one such life storm. I felt as if it would bring my entire world crashing down, leaving me alone and abandoned. Many times I doubted. Many times I was full of fear. Many times I felt utter frustration and dismay in the face of chaos. But through it all, I managed to persevere. My perseverance led me to many things, one of them being a niche in a new career. Through this experience, I learned that people search far and wide for a source of hope during the middle of their storms. As you read, you will come across many of the imperfections and missteps I experienced along the way. My fervent desire is that you will walk away from reading this with hope and a deepened belief in your ability to weather your storms.

When I reminisce on my experiences, I am filled with inspiration for the future because I look at where I was, and see where I am now. All of the growth, all of the change, and all of the challenge has brought me to an incredible turning point, despite the burdensome incidents that took place. I hope to be able to inspire and equip you with the tools necessary for your own story of victory. You *should* believe in yourself. And I'm going to show you why and how.

Chapter One

An Unexpected Change of Pace

When it rains, it pours

- Morton Salt Company

It was the morning after the accident, and I still felt numb. The sky was gray and empty. A dark haze blanketed the tree line where I stood. There was not even a car driving by to interrupt the silence I felt within my soul. I walked over to talk with Christian, the framing crew leader for the home we were building. I noticed that with every step I took, I felt like I was trudging through thick, dark mud. Christian made eye contact and greeted me enthusiastically as I approached. We had planned to meet that morning to discuss job-site problems he and his crew were running into, so he immediately started asking me questions and brainstorming. All the while, his crew was hard at work on the roof trusses above us. I was still in such a state of shock that I kept my head bowed, and didn't return his eye or respond.

He paused heavily in the middle of his sentence, picking up on my distress from my posture. As my gaze lifted to meet his, I felt nauseated by a feeling of panic that swept through my entire body. Tears began rolling down my face as I mumbled, "There was an accident. Tim is in the hospital."

By that point, the work of the framing crew had slowed. Each one of them began holstering their tools and looking at us in confusion, as they registered something was amiss. Noticing my discomfort, Christian quickly guided me away from their scrutiny toward the shelter of the work truck.

"What on earth do you mean? Is Tim okay?" he asked with confusion and worry evident all over his face.

I struggled to find the words, annoyed with myself for being unable to speak. Finally, I mumbled angrily, "This is why you don't see women on the job site; they're too emotional!" I continued, "Tim was in a wreck and was rushed to the hospital but I don't know much more than that, I'm sorry. I don't know what to do!" As I could feel myself fighting down a rising wave of panic.

A moment of silence passed. I attempted to regain composure by asking him, "What was it you needed to run by me?"

He looked at me with the same concern as before. This time, there was a gentle look on his face that made me feel like I could relax. As I took a deep breath and tried to calm myself from the fearful state of anguish I was drowning in, he simply said, "Don't worry."

"Great," I thought to myself. "A guy telling a woman not to worry is just what I need to hear right now." But I didn't dare say a word out loud, as I was still consumed with emotion. Christian continued, "It will all work out and it will all be okay. Don't stress about these other issues, it's not like we haven't come across them before. We'll get them figured out and it will be fine."

There was a lot of information swirling around in my head that I gathered from this encounter. Of course, there are not many people who want to be told not to worry when indeed, there seem to be plenty of legitimate reasons to do so. Starting something new can become a daunting task. And at the same time, this task can also be exciting. Yet, this excitement can quickly turn into a stressful event. Especially when you suddenly become in charge of so many individuals and projects (that you hardly know anything about) as you struggle to even find the confidence that you can lead them in the right direction. There are several factors that make the thought of displaying emotion as a female in a male-dominated industry feel terrifying. If I were to show fear or concern about a situation, would anyone have faith that I could effectively handle it? Would I be perceived as incompetent or lesser than others? As my leadership role increased and the reality of my co-worker's absence set in, these were all thoughts circling in my head.

My career, just like that of many others in early 2020, seemed to be falling apart right in front of me. Almost overnight, my income was cut in half and there seemed to be a lot of uncertainty that surrounded the average working American. I was confronted by the need to adapt and find new survival techniques and do so uncomfortably fast. I was quickly flung out of my professional comfort zone in health and wellness into a field I knew nothing about…construction. Everything in the world was moving so quickly that I didn't have time to consider the significance of my decisions within a job market and economy that was so uncertain.

For years, my area of expertise existed in the field of Exercise Science and personal training. I had invested so much time and knowledge into achieving various certifications ranging from a movement specialist to athletic performance to excel at personal training for fifteen years. The feeling of being ill-equipped and out of my element in this new field was disconcerting, and that was before my co-worker's accident elevated me to supervisor status. If you have ever been in a similar situation, you are likely familiar with how shocking and anxiety-inducing stepping out of your own well-known territory can be.

For me, construction was not an industry I had considered an option as a woman, let alone during such a fast-paced housing market boom. To make matters worse, the only time I had available to learn this new trade was through hands-on experience as each issue in turn presented itself in front of me.

So there I stood with the framing crew leader; a personal trainer, now on a construction site with a clipboard in hand, unable to read building plans, and suddenly in charge of a job that demanded I be confident and in control in a situation where I felt overwhelmed and uncertain about the depth of responsibilities I inherited. In the blink of an eye, having no construction experience, I was now managing over a hundred subcontractors. I was building a subdivision of custom homes, each home in various stages of completion, in addition to managing other building sites located throughout the area.

    At this point, you could be wondering how I survived. Or, how did a woman in a brand new career field with no formal training or education inconceivably build an entire subdivision and more? How did she manage to face her fears head-on while simultaneously tackling anxieties in an unknown and constantly changing work environment? And how did she manage to do all of this while battling a high-demand housing market expansion coupled with unprecedented material and labor shortages?

    This is a story of my struggle and subsequent triumph. I hope that by reading this, you find encouragement for your own challenges that you may be facing or will eventually come across one day. Within the chapters to follow, I will be laying out a blueprint containing the fundamental insights of humility, leadership, and relationship building that I learned along the way. This will allow you to effectively approach any intimidating situation with confident resilience.

By sharing my story, my aim is to help you battle through your own experiences with the new and terrifying. I hope to inspire you in the same way others inspired me and gave me the courage to seize the opportunities in front of me.

Chapter Two

With Change Comes Resilience

Courage is not the absence of fear, courage is fear walking.

- Susan David, Emotional Resilience

So there I sat, numb, and my heart pounding. I had just begun working with a custom home builder. I knew the transition into a new industry wasn't going to be easy, but it was starting to become fun for me to learn so many new things. I enjoyed being part of the creative thought process when it came to solving issues. Each day on the job site was always different than the last and I was beginning to adjust to the change. Then, there was a day I experienced a gut-wrenching feeling that something wasn't right.

The accident happened late one afternoon as I was finishing up details for a screened-in porch with the carpentry crew. I was waiting for a phone call from Tim, who was supposed to be on his way back from town to drop off the remaining material we needed for the project. We were ahead of schedule, so everyone was relaxed and discussing their plans for the upcoming weekend.

"Well this is a little strange," I said out loud to the crew. "Tim should have been back by now, but I guess we'll have to finish this tomorrow."

"I wouldn't worry about it," the head carpenter assured me. "We can always come back first thing tomorrow before heading over to your other house."

"Ok, cool. Guess I'll see y'all tomorrow then," I said as I packed up my things and began to leave the job site.

The work day was ending on a good note, so I tried not to think any further about the fact that it was so odd I still had not heard back from Tim as I was walking to my vehicle. Moments later, I received a phone call. It was my boss. His kids normally had baseball practice at that time, so I thought it strange that he would be calling me but I answered anyway.

"Hey Matt, how's it going?" I answered hesitantly.

"Hey Morgan, have you heard from Tim today?" he asked with a strange uncertainty in his voice that I didn't recognize.

"Not since this morning. I've been waiting for him most of the day to come back with the material we needed to finish out here," I said as I grew increasingly intrigued as to why he was calling me.

"Well," he fumbled to say with a long pause, "I talked to his son. Tim was in an accident and he's being taken by a CareFlight helicopter to the hospital." Matt expressed intense anguish in his voice. *This can't be real,* as I thought to myself.

    Tim was the only job-site teacher I had in construction up to that point. The dreadful phone call I received that afternoon was crushing to my spirit. Tim had experienced a massive stroke that led to a head-on car collision. I was devastated by the news. I instantly became disoriented, and all my thoughts were consumed with worry about him and his family. I was baffled by the news and I could hardly believe this was real life. I was already in completely uncharted territory, and now, I was alone. If you have ever received a phone call like this, you can relate to the overwhelming feelings that seem to immediately flood the entire body with apprehension about all of the unknowns that are about to take place. I seemed to be stuck in a haze of angst.

    Being a female in a male-dominated workforce, I felt like I was a stranger. I immediately attached a sense of comfort to Tim on the job-site as he showed me the roles of different people and how everything operated. This comfort was heightened by Tim's rigorous sense of order. There was a strategic flow to how Tim chose to run his job-sites. He had a detail-oriented schedule, and he was never worried much about anything. Easy, in control, and laid back, never sweating the small stuff. Tim is the type of guy who can make friends with anyone on the job-site. He will often go out of his way to say hello to anyone who is present and make sure that they have everything they need. He was extremely knowledgeable about the construction process, making him both an effective and patient teacher. Nothing seemed to brighten his day more than having the opportunity to teach a willing person.

Even prior to Tim's accident, managing multiple job-sites had already become stressful. The exploding housing market, driven by an increased desire of people to work from home, place a lot of demand on the construction industry. Families were rushing to the picturesque view of the countryside to experience the benefits of quiet and quaint living, leaving their former bustling style of city life far behind. This increased demand drastically, and coupled with the global shutdown meant that supply chain disruptions were frequent. Abnormal material shortages quickly followed. Manufacturing delays were impossible to anticipate, and the way job-sites were managed in the past was now irrelevant. These curveballs became daily occurrences that added to the stress of learning a new field as a manager.

When Tim's accident occurred, I was suddenly left to manage everything by myself with just a notepad and a few tools in my bag. Tim's unexpected absence made me feel like I was way in over my head and far outside of my element.

With a minimal amount of experience, the weight of the situation became a heavy burden to carry. Now, more than ever, I felt like I didn't belong and that I was not going to be able to build all of the homes on my own. Managing every detail of each custom home, as well as over one hundred subcontractors, while maintaining favorable relationships with the manufacturers and clients, became enough to skyrocket my anxiety and confusion to a new level. Despite the horrific news of Tim's absence and the daily bombardment of unexpected problems, I still had to maintain cohesive schedules for everyone to continue working in and out of each house smoothly.

MAKING A CHOICE

With everything that I was facing, I had a few choices that I needed to make. I could choose to allow myself to be consumed by my own fear and inexperience, and thus give credibility to my self-doubts and the doubts of others, especially given that I'm a female in a historically predominantly male workforce. Or, I could choose to accept my limitations and strive to learn and improve as I went while accepting that I would make mistakes. This was not a one-person job. With so many different moving parts and people scattered throughout the county we were building in, I was convinced that it was nearly impossible for a single individual to maintain their sanity while keeping track of the ongoing chaos. Managing solo at this level created a significant risk of missing a detail that could have devastating repercussions.

    A common barrier within various industries is the fact that in many cultures older male counterparts tend to be respected more than females. I was determined to overcome that hurdle by showing that I was patient and willing to learn, despite my knowledge gaps. I wanted to show them I belonged in this role for a reason. I chose to lead with the notion and belief that if you show them how competent a woman can be, they can start thinking all women are capable.

When specifically referring to cultural norms, there is a gender bias that tends to pose a huge issue for both men and women alike. This has led to a lot of stagnation and unhappiness throughout the US-based workforce. Think of it this way: there is a massive untapped labor market when it comes to women working in construction who are not only capable individuals but who can bring forth an entirely different skill set to benefit the industry as a whole. If women can bring increased productivity to the industry, it can strengthen our entire economy. Regardless of this fact, it is evident that women are not as encouraged as their male counterparts to enter the construction industry.

Of all the construction workers in the US, women comprise only 11% (1). Even fewer is the number of women working on the front lines of job-sites as superintendents or on-site project manager roles, making up about 1 for every 100 employees in the field.

Despite the troubling numbers, the industry is not doomed to be stuck in the past. There is, in fact, hope for those companies willing to recruit women and benefit from their work in construction. Studies reveal that the most gender-diverse companies are more likely to achieve above-average profitability compared to those companies with less diversification (2).

    To say I felt like an outlier would be an understatement, but I still had a choice to make: minimize the fears I clung to and face the unknown with grit, determination, and self-confidence. I had to learn to trust that I was more resilient than the unlucky circumstances surrounding me. And even hesitantly at the time, I chose to trust my determination to succeed and lean on those around me who were willing to support and guide me through what turned out to be one of the toughest seasons of my life.

EMBRACING CHANGE

When change occurs, the rules of engagement are different. The strategy used yesterday may be obsolete today. I fully accepted that I had so much new information to take in and needed to evolve quickly in order to stay afloat. I embraced the realization that the world around me was changing quicker than I could keep up with, especially during a global shutdown. Many industries during that time of the pandemic were slowing down and some nearly coming to a halt, but the construction industry experienced the opposite effect. Contractors and builders alike were buried deep with the rising demand.

I quickly noticed that I had to embrace my ability to pivot and work around the complexities present to me despite still trying to grasp the fundamentals of construction. I decided I also had to embrace the notion that I could not do anything about this changing environment. In doing so, I repeatedly observed that so many people were struggling to figure out how they could continue doing the same thing they always did. Very few people recognized this moment in time as an opportunity. I knew that it would become imperative for me to stay focused so that I and my projects could keep moving forward despite the vast amount of struggle around me.

To succeed in a new or unknown environment, I felt it was necessary to first address the inherent fears and uncertainties I was surrounded by. At that time, there was no shortage of anxiety floating around so this practice required diligent effort and concentration every single day. And if I were to allow that fear to control me during that time alone supervising the job sites, the result could have been catastrophic for myself and the people under my supervision. No one wants to purposefully experience the negative effects of their actions, or in this case, inaction.

    Every home that we were building could have come to a complete halt. That meant there was no other choice but to accept and embrace the change ahead of me, something I so deeply wanted to avoid. Yet, what I discovered was, the further I dove into embracing the change happening around me, the more certain I became in my abilities to thrive within that environment. With my focus narrowed in, it allowed me to accomplish important assignments without regard to my fear leading the way or preventing me from making progress. Accepting change and tackling adversity by moving with the change proved to be so effective, that it gave me an upper hand in providing me with the capacity to stay task-oriented to continue moving forward during a less-than-ideal season.

Fully accepting that I had a lot of adversity to overcome made it easier for me to evolve within my work surroundings and succeed in something I had never done before. It allowed me to demonstrate a remarkable ability to tactically and strategically process information that may not have otherwise been considered. Even with no shortage of tradesmen around me who were busy complaining and fighting against the inevitable changes, I was able to continue leading. Accepting this reality allowed me to interact with fresh ideas and do what few others thought was possible. Before I knew it, little by little, every aspect of the home-building process began to progress forward. By accepting my reality, I was able to anticipate disturbances within our production and comprehend the effects more clearly so that the negative impact would be less significant, thus overcoming adversity.

Despite being long past the days of conquistadors, I find their story of burning the ships upon arrival to a New World still relevant. History reports that Hernan Cortez, one of the most renowned Spanish crusaders, was infamous for ordering his men to burn the ships by which they arrived after discovering new land (3). This act sent a clear message to his crew: there is no turning back and no option for retreat. What I find relevant from his story and what I decided to adopt as a leader, is the notion that once I decide to fully move forward with a decision, I have to abandon all other options. As leaders, unless all other options are removed from the table, how will you gain full commitment from those under your guidance? Once committed to a decision, leaving the door slightly open behind you tends to beg the question of whether you are fully invested in that choice and potentially leaves more room for error.

As I briefly mentioned before, not everyone on your team will be keen on embracing change. For some, it may take longer for them to see the benefits of change and be open to it. Others may completely reject the idea of change altogether. It was very important in those chaotic moments to not let discouragement from others affect my decisions and path going forward. Even though other people's resistance to change created more work for me at the moment, it still set me up for success in the long run. It was a gamble, to say the least, but it was also vital that I still progress forward and not allow the struggle that others were experiencing to affect me. This became easier when I committed myself to operate on the job site as what I call a producer.

Being a producer means that even though I am unqualified, I reject that as an excuse as to why I can't succeed within my circumstances. By fully committing to a decision I made, without giving myself another option, I was able to accomplish what needed to get done and find creative ways around obstacles that may have normally halted someone else's progress. That same mindset allowed me to focus on making sure the work was completed in a manner that exceeded the expected standard, no matter what.

PRACTICING RESILIENCE

The American Psychological Association defines resilience as: the process and outcome of successfully adapting to difficult or challenging life experiences, especially through mental, emotional, and behavioral

flexibility and adjustment to external and internal demands (4). For me, practicing and developing resilience requires awareness and acknowledgment of what is in my control, and what is not. For example, a day in construction is never the same as the previous day. It's an environment in a constant state of change, both good and bad.

This realization indicated that I had to practice becoming resilient to the ever-changing environment, and in essence, constantly adapt and adjust the ways I did things to meet the current demands. I did this by recognizing that my environment is greatly influenced by the application of problem-solving skills.

In construction we like to say, it is necessary to preemptively solve problems even when there are no current problems to solve as inevitably they will arise. The more prepared you are upfront, the more time and money you can save in the moment, and in the long run. I have come to learn that it is a good practice to create numerous alternate road maps in order to mitigate other problems that will inevitably arise. When one issue occurs, the issue is rarely localized. It can either be a fun guessing game or an exhausting task to trace how far one seemingly small issue has greatly impacted multiple areas. In these scenarios, mental and behavioral flexibility is a must to survive.

In other words, anticipating and planning a substantial number of steps ahead of the current state of the project would inevitably ease the pain of dealing with an unexpected issue that I had no control over. This act alone would help lessen the negative impact and surprise factors involved with complex projects that were already under high stress and rigid timelines.

For instance, weather-related issues in construction can cause huge delays and create a list of unintended problems. Those weather-related issues usually need fixing, and refixing, and oftentimes they need to be solved immediately. Knowing this, and planning for its potential negative effects on any given project, I could practice my skills of resilience by pivoting and redirecting efforts so that other work would still be accomplished while keeping stress to a minimum. This ability to pivot project focus would greatly lessen a logistical nightmare with schedules and subcontractors working against the clock to complete their tasks. And even though surprises happen, it was an alleviating feeling for me to know that most of them were already anticipated by having thorough plans of action in place.

When continually adapting to new and difficult situations, another important tactic I learned was taking a deep dive into my own understanding of what was being presented to me. Since I no longer had Tim as a buffer to explain in detail why an issue was so significant, it became highly imperative for me to understand the root causes of the issues happening so that I could effectively manage and address them. Without this full understanding, important details can be overlooked, and no one has the time or desire to fix something twice. As I further developed my understanding, I saw an opportunity to formulate new ways of thinking and tackling issues most tradesmen had never seen before.

Einstein is quoted as saying, "No problems can be solved from the same consciousness that created it." For me this meant allowing my perspective to shift can elicit an evolved or even more detailed way of problem-solving. The fact that I had less experience than many of the tradesmen, and had a fresh outsider's perspective proved increasingly valuable. Having the ability to approach a workplace issue with a fresh perspective can lead to an incredibly productive environment.

    The construction industry is filled with experienced tradesmen who are accustomed to getting things done in a specific tried-and-true manner. It was daunting to communicate to the workers that maybe a different approach could work better instead. As I toyed with this idea that I had something of value to offer, I continued to gain confidence that my fresh perspective in conjunction with their time-tested experience could result in better production. And it did. I want to encourage those who may have different views, to share them, as you may not know how helpful they could prove to be.

However, practicing and developing resilience to a changing environment does take time, trial, and error. Everyone has the ability to learn how to conquer and/or manage their fears when they put these tools into practice. Part of this practice also includes leaning into your intuition and the strengths that you and the individuals around you already possess. The importance of remaining open and accepting of the evolving world around you will only continue to pay off over time as you learn and grow into your abilities.

LIFE ADVICE

I was given a piece of advice, that even to this day, its pure simplicity still resonates with me. It became a foundational element of guidance for me as I tried to comprehend the intensity that surrounded me. Not only was I overwhelmed by all that I was in charge of amidst Tim's absence, but I was also equally as terrified of letting people down. I viewed letting people down as equal to failing at my job, and at the same time, there was not a chance I was going to allow the idea to emerge that women were not suited for the tough stuff. Despite my constant state of anxiety, I was determined to prove that women can be successful in this industry.

With the chaos and confusion, I found myself often forgetting what was said to me. I was still learning basic construction terminology, and without this simple piece of advice, I know I would have been lost. The advice given was to write everything down. Literally everything. Write it *all* down. For some, this may seem trivial, but if you have ever been there yourself then you understand how important and life-changing this can really be. As one can imagine I was not very impressed at first, but at that point, what did I have to lose? So I decided to go with it.

Not long after taking this piece of advice to heart, I became known around my job sites for always having a notepad in hand. I wrote down every detail, no matter how seemingly small and insignificant. My notetaking skills were present for every meeting, every phone call, and every inspection that was held. It seemed as if overnight my fears and anxieties were lifted, and I gained a profound sense of relief in my work. What surprised me even more, was that it was becoming apparent that my subcontractors appreciated my efforts. Making this conscious effort every day sent the message that I respected their time and was diligent in keeping with my eagerness to learn despite being overwhelmed. To me, it also showed that I belonged. It proved that I, too, was capable.

Construction was not second nature to me as it was for the tradesmen I worked alongside. A lot of it still isn't. But I wholeheartedly believe that showing up with a willingness to learn creates an environment that softens the barriers that anyone might face as a new worker in a particular field. It can also enhance communication, as people tend to be inspired by honesty and openness.

I was understood and accepted for who I was in that season of growth as a result of my willingness to learn and the honesty I presented. I was often amazed at the empathy and understanding I received and *I still* marvel at that experience.

Chapter two takeaways

- You do not have to know it all to begin, you just have to start.
- Trust in your gut that you have been given the innate ability to figure it out as you go.
- Write everything down!
- Do not let the fear of cultural norms stop you from exploring something new.

- Lean in on those around you.

- Develop and practice environmental awareness (i.e. taking into account the needs of those around you but not forgetting about the physical environment as it may also require something of you).

- Preemptively plan for possible hiccups to make life easier not just for yourself, but for those around you and how they operate in your presence.

- Alleviate pressure on yourself by making your knowledge gaps known. This takes courage, but the resilient person can recognize self-admittance as the bravest form of courage. When you make these boundaries known, this allows you to mitigate otherwise potential unknown expectations that could cause setbacks.

Chapter Three

How to Lead When You Don't Know What You Are Doing

Hardships often prepare ordinary people for an extraordinary destiny.

- C.S. Lewis

Armed with renewed self-confidence that came from writing everything down, I felt like I was ready to effectively tackle the complexities of construction. The more I understood that I didn't need to know it all in order to successfully complete this subdivision, I began to thrive and move forward with confidence. It felt like I finally realized my management potential. This was empowering to me, especially as the only woman on the job site. I continued to learn how to cultivate these abilities so that I could better support the people under my supervision.

One of the first challenges to my new growth in self-assurance was the priority list I had to keep as a supervisor. In an industry where everything is a priority, the list established tasks that demanded immediate attention, as well as those that could be more flexible in their time of completion. Increased productivity increases profit, and without being led by the tyranny of the urgent, I could keep production moving in a timely manner, which was essential to our environmental circumstances. This priority list aided in keeping my focus from home to home (job-site to job-site) while also being able to clearly and concisely keep track of material or logistical complications.

REMEMBER TO BREATHE

One of the first times I had to put my newfound crisis management skills to the test came on an unassuming morning. As I walked up to the multiple job sites, I noticed the numerous tradesmen already hard at work as their trucks filled the driveways and flooded into the street. Each home was swarming with people working on houses that were all at different stages of completion in their construction. One house had drilling for a well system while another had the HVAC subcontractors finishing up their final system checks. At another house, the plumbers were installing their kitchen and bathroom fixtures, while shingles were being installed on the roof of another. The carpentry crew was split between two houses, adding the finishing touches on one and installing the kitchen cabinets in the other.

As I continued observing this hive of activity, I was accompanied by loud diverse power equipment noises echoing from every direction. Within minutes of my arrival that morning, the master plumber greeted me with uncertainty in his voice. "You're not going to want to hear this," he said. My stomach churned. Meanwhile, the head carpenter working in the house next door had noticed our meeting. He quickly hung his tools and walked over to join our conversation. As he approached he began talking loudly over the heavy machinery; "We've got some problems I need you to take a look at sooner rather than later."

And there it was. With the bombardment of bad news, a wave of insecurity rushed over me again as I was plagued by imposter syndrome-like thoughts. They were all looking at me. *Problems are manifesting left and right and I'm supposed to be the person to solve all of them...but how?* Thoughts continued to flood my mind. *What am I doing here? What role am I pretending to fill?*

"I don't have all these answers," I mumbled inaudibly as I stood lifeless in front of the carpenter and plumber who were having their own conversation over a smoke break about whose problem was worse. At this point, it had been weeks since my coworker's accident and there was still no update on his chances of recovery. A small part of me had been hoping he would be able to come back before the big issues started to emerge for the reassurance that his return would bring, not only to myself but also to everyone else. But here I was, being peppered with questions that I had no clue how to answer or even attempt to solve. There could be no delay; I had to field the questions and find solutions.

As I took a long deep breath before finally responding, a resounding voice emanated in my head about the circumstance I found myself in, *"You've got this, I'm proud of you!"*

This voice was comforting in its significance as I began to recall a recent conversation I had with Tim, who was making his way through physical therapy re-learning how to walk. He reassured me how hard he was working and that he would return to the field as soon as he was able. Tim understood the burden of being in this environment alone and the immense pressures of navigating the pandemic. As Tim was doing all that he could, I, in turn, reassured him I had this taken care of, and the only thing that mattered was his improvement so he could return home to his family. Tim believed in me to take care of things. And with that thought, my doubts began to dissipate.

"Okay," I said, taking yet another deep breath as I looked at both the carpenter and plumber still standing in front of me, "Tell me in detail what each of you is facing so I can figure out the best plan of action."

UNDERSTANDING LEADERSHIP

This wasn't the first time I was faced with more than one crucial complex issue to overcome paired with fast-approaching deadlines. But this was the first time that I truly began to understand that leadership is about taking ownership as well as initiative, especially in moments of crisis.

I'd never envisioned myself in this type of leadership role, but when faced with high demand and few options for error, with a lot of opportunity for criticism, few others would be rushing in to fill the position. How else would this sub-division get completed? My boss and other co-worker were flooded with their own projects and fires to put out in the office, which meant that this was my responsibility to take on. The very moment that Tim was absent from the job site left everyone relying solely on me to make those executive decisions and follow through with every single one. With Tim gone, sitting in the commanding chair meant I had to accept the good, the bad, and the ugly part of each of these challenges whether I was prepared for them or not.

When we think about the most remarkable leaders in history, most of them were thrown into leadership positions before they felt ready. If I wanted to dare to be different, as a competent woman in a historically labeled "man's job", and prove to myself and those around me that I was capable, I could not shy away from crises that fell upon me and forced me time and again out of my comfort zone. At the time, I knew one thing for certain: if I avoided the challenges presented to me, I would regress a great deal and miss the vital opportunity to prove that women are capable of making this type of impact. I knew I had to grow and evolve in order to succeed. So for me, that meant there was no option to stay stagnant. Making a conscious choice to accept full ownership over the obstacles presented is inevitably how leaders pull through burdensome moments. There has to be someone willing to take a risk and make tough decisions.

Since no one at this point could afford to lose any more time beyond what the pandemic delays had caused, it left me with no other choice. I had to become a leader, and I chose to lead despite uncertainty and risk. I chose to lead with courage over my discomfort. My entire world was uncomfortable, so what else did I have to lose? Of course, I had my doubts and still didn't know if I was up for the challenge, but I had to try for the sake of everyone involved.

As time progressed, I found there wasn't another person to whom I could go to receive advice or encouragement about how to handle my new workload. There was no one I could open up to about the immense stress I was under, and there were very few people who could fully understand the complexities and consequences of the decisions I was responsible for. That was a lonely position to be in. But, aside from the negative and fearful emotions, I was continually experiencing, there was a more powerful feeling that I failed to perceive. That feeling was significance. I was an important and vital leader of the team.

STAY CURIOUS

Having no prior knowledge about what it takes to be a leader and how to successfully manage over a hundred workers who are producing a custom product, I discovered that leadership is a skill. And, it is a skill that I cultivated through endless trial and error. More importantly, it was also helpful to realize that leadership is a skill that can be learned and developed by anyone. This realization aided in my confidence to lead, and despite being alone in this role for an undetermined amount of time, it allowed me to make the conscious choice to show up and deliver, regardless of the fatiguing circumstances.

We do not always have the good will of choosing our misfortunes. I was constantly forced to choose pursuits that may not have otherwise been considered by someone more experienced than myself. And within this new angle, I stumbled across another technique that I believed was not only powerful but severely underrated throughout the industry. As a female working in construction, this simple technique displayed an impactful point of view that provided me the opportunity to work swiftly and effectively. It allowed me to make better choices for my projects and lean further into my development as a leader.

The technique that helped guide me through adversity time and again was displaying curiosity. No matter how uncomfortable a situation, I stayed curious by always asking questions. It seems trivial, but the effects became profound throughout the workforce. No matter who my questions were directed toward, I learned to distinguish the distinct yet subtle difference between asking a tradesman *why* – just for the sake of it and risk being perceived as if I was questioning the integrity of his work – versus phrasing my questions in a way that allowed me to understand his entire process and the effects his methodology would have on myself, the timeline, and everyone else involved.

    I noticed a significant difference in the feedback I received when I led with pure curiosity and an open mind. Choosing to be actively receptive to the responses I received (whether I already knew the outcome or not), helped me to elicit a better end product and a more positive, productive work environment. The temptation to point out an obvious problem felt overpowering when I had deadlines to meet. If I was not 100% sure that it was a critical issue, I erred on the side of curiosity rather than certainty.

I like what Neil deGrasse Tyson said about this type of approach: "One of the great challenges in this world is knowing enough about a subject to think you're right, but not enough about the subject to know you're wrong."

There are many scenarios that could have led to a less-than-desirable outcome for everyone, both physically and mentally. Showing up and issuing orders like a drill sergeant would have exasperated the tradesmen. Blindly giving orders is not the mark of a good leader nor would it have been an effective strategy to take. I wanted to show the tradesmen that I cared about them and their quality of work, both of which greatly influenced the end product. I chose to show up on the job-site with open-mindedness and genuine curiosity. I made it my daily goal to ask the tradesmen to further explain their methodology on an issue so that I could better understand the process in the larger building scheme. By allowing my curiosity to drive conversations with various tradesmen, I was able to enrich my level of understanding in different fields. This in turn elevated the performance of the tradesmen under my supervision because they wanted to demonstrate excellent performance while they taught me about their process.

    The perception may be that this method would delay progress, but I experienced the opposite. When it became apparent to the tradesmen that they and their concerns were valued and understood, they took pride in their work, and their work pace accelerated. I realized that if I helped each team member feel valued at some level, they were likely to be more motivated to accomplish the tasks efficiently.

    I believe it benefits everyone in a working environment when gaps in one's knowledge are readily admitted. Having this awareness of our own intellectual deficiencies can foster dynamic collaboration by providing a vital exchange of information. This information, in turn, can help us to be more successful in any industry. In the context of solving problems, failure to be curious can result in incomplete solutions. Remaining curious requires focusing on the nature of the problem before considering a solution. Curiosity and knowledge-building can grow simultaneously. The more we know, the more we want to know.

When we are curious, the brain can become primed and ready to learn and retain information. Even so, displaying any level of curiosity can feel uncomfortable because it requires uncertainty and vulnerability. I love what one of my favorite researchers and authors on shame and vulnerability, Brené Brown, says, "Vulnerability is the birthplace of innovation, creativity, and change."

BUILDING TRUST

The tradesmen knew that I cared how things were accomplished by my methods of listening to understand and asking questions without being pretentious. It became less difficult to ask questions that I felt were hard or potentially insignificant, as the relationships and trust developed. The improved communication also assisted in maximizing resources and time, whereas previously, it might have been wasted. As was true in many other professional fields, starting a new job in construction during the beginning of a global shutdown was a daunting task. As building material prices continued to skyrocket, it became imperative for my team and I to devise innovative ways to problem-solve.

  Another attribute of being a successful leader that I learned in my 'hands-on leadership training school' was making it a point to incorporate the expertise of others. Valuable leaders understand that they may not possess all the tools to accomplish their goals. Therefore, putting their people in positions to thrive assists the leaders to be more successful.

My inexperience with the home construction process could have caused major issues with the subcontractors, had I not learned how to use it to my advantage. Recognizing the professional knowledge and skills that the subcontractors possessed, and allowing them to thrive while making sure they worked in unison, was a highly effective solution. I showed them I respected their skills and experience, and in return, they demonstrated respect for what I had to do as the project leader. This eased my anxieties as well as helped to increase the trust between myself and the subcontractors. I learned a powerful lesson: people are most motivated when they follow leaders they *want* to follow, not that they *have* to follow.

For example, I did not need to know how to frame the roof of a house. But I did need to rely on the expertise of those who could when I was presented with something that in actuality didn't line up with the theoretical design on paper. It has become common knowledge in this type of work that it's necessary to anticipate confronting all types of issues that were not originally projected. Anyone experienced in fieldwork will know what I mean when I say to expect that things will not always translate from behind the computer screen as they are projected to in real-life situations.

If you want to make an impact, or if you are simply aiming to prove that you are capable as a leader within your environment, then deciding to step up and get your hands dirty with your crew from time to time can be a wise move. I believe that when you're capable, there is no substitute for leading by example. In my experience, strapping on a tool belt or picking up a shovel when crews were short-handed, or running behind schedule, instantly granted me an elevated level of respect and trust from the subcontractors. A leader who is willing to engage in the same activities as their fellow worker creates a culture of trust by doing so. No longer is that leader viewed simply as giving orders, but as someone who is giving guidance with a clear understanding of the challenges being faced.

When you talk about a deadline and have personally worked frantically to meet that deadline, the tone of the conversation changes. Of course, there was the practical bonus of having an extra pair of hands to make the work move faster and minimize the delays we faced.

The last work environment I thought I would ever be in was construction. I have been a part of many intimidating situations before, especially situations in which I was the only female present. So the feelings of being part of the unknown construction environment were familiar. But to arrive on a job site day after day with the unnerving awareness that I was working as a leader was frightening. Add my level of inexperience, and that made the entire bit terrifying on a massive scale.

Every imaginable label of fear and vulnerability, I experienced daily. Trying to show up confidently as a new leader without being overcome by the immense fear I felt was incredibly burdensome, but with time and loads of practice, I eventually found my way. My fears were largely relieved by that process of building trust with people I had not previously encountered. This in turn allowed me to thrive in my leadership role and exceed my expectations of myself as well as those that others had of me.

In that pressured environment, I could either grow or wilt, and I chose to grow by maintaining genuine curiosity. That growth did not happen without the incredible people surrounding me, because they provided me with a strong foundation of support. It took time and effort to build that foundation, but once it was established, every problem seemed conquerable. That is when I found the measure of a true leader: being able to rise to the occasion and rally the people around you when the pressure is at its peak.

Chapter Three Takeaways

- Building trust with those around you can play out to your advantage.
- Don't be afraid to strap on tools and get dirty.
- Set the ego aside and remember to stay curious.
- Genuine curiosity for learning can serve as a great leadership tool.

Chapter Four

Learning to Adapt and Evolve

Success is stumbling from failure to failure with no loss of enthusiasm.

- Winston Churchill

Have you ever considered the notion that humans are the creatures most capable of changing their environment so that they can thrive in it? Yet, despite this unrivaled ability to shape our environment, we often possess a reluctance to exercise that power. Instead, we grow comfortable in our surroundings and lose our sense of awareness of how our environment affects us. In this chapter, I want to share the importance of becoming critically aware of how to change your environment and how to increase your adaptability skills, which can be of great benefit to yourself and those around you. I will also explain why I believe having a strong sense of belonging within an environment can play a significant role in your success and the achievements of those around you.

DEVELOPING AWARENESS

When we become accustomed to doing things in a certain manner, it becomes difficult to admit when our methodology has become obsolete or inadequate. With so many companies and industries experiencing ongoing disruptions to their usual ways of doing business, there is an increased need for individuals to become critically aware of their environments, which in turn prepares them to effectively manage ongoing disruptions. No one is simply born with this type of critical self-awareness. It takes a great deal of courage to build it, being that it is a skill that needs to be learned, refined, and strengthened over time. This improved awareness can increase workplace productivity, decrease stress, and heighten flexibility both for individuals and the organizations within which they work. I believe it is important to recognize the need to strengthen our own critical awareness skills, especially within new environments, in an effort to learn how to effectively plan for potential glitches in the workplace.

Engaging in the skill of being aware of your surroundings can firsthand ease the discomfort of change when it inevitably happens, making it more manageable. Failure to refine this important skill can lead to unwarranted chaos, distrust in leadership or the end goal, loss of time, and unnecessary frustration between individuals, to name just a few. One method I have found to achieve balance within my changing environment is staying proactive and constantly preparing for ongoing challenges so that I am more adept at making effective changes on the spot.

Due to being critically aware of my environment and the people within it, it was very easy for me to pick up on their skepticism when I was first introduced to the construction sites and got to know the tradesmen. After all, only 9.9% of all construction workers are female (5). If I had been blind to their leery attitudes, I may not have gotten as far as I did. Finding my place in the world of construction was not easy, especially at first when I began feeling out of my element. Engaging critical awareness skills helped ease the adjustment, specifically when I was put on the hot seat to problem-solve and manage right out of the gate. It also helped me recognize how much I still had to learn and gave me the drive to prove my worth and value as a woman in a field where I was in the minority.

There were countless situations where my ability to adapt became essential in order to prevent halting the entire building process, which was already under a jam-packed schedule. There was one instance in particular that catapulted these abilities which coincidently for myself and a few others, will stand out for quite some time.

Before diving into the circumstance, let me first explain the lumber configuration of a typical custom home rooftop. A rooftop usually consists of a few peaks that are divided into many individual triangles. These triangles are called roof trusses. All trusses are prefabricated by a manufacturer and each one is specifically engineered to carry a certain load on the home, which means each truss belongs in an exact location on the roof. The equipment commonly used to mobilize and set roof trusses is a crane. The semi-truck delivering the trusses drops them as close to the home as possible, so the crane can reach them. Roof trusses can span anywhere from 40 to 80 feet in length, so attempting to carry them by hand can be a nearly impossible task.

    On this particular day shortly before his accident, Tim and I received a call early one morning alerting us that the semi-truck delivering our roof trusses was having trouble navigating the streets within the gated community where we were building. This was a tightly-packed bustling neighborhood that had painfully narrow streets. If two vehicles were approaching one another and a trash can was protruding just a few feet into the street beyond a mailbox, it would be hit or knocked over by a side-view mirror. This scenario eventually caused the semi truck's inability to maneuver within the narrow confines of the road, leaving us no other option but to drop the entire truss package, containing 72 roof trusses, in the middle of the street.

Tim and I immediately realized that blocking the road and numerous driveways due to the length of the trusses would be a huge aggravation if we didn't adapt to a new plan and move fast. In a typical situation, a semi-truck can drop the roof trusses in the yard or the construction driveway. Since our environment did not allow a truck of this size with lumber protruding about 10 feet off the rear of the truck – to maneuver in any way that would have been helpful – we were left with the worst-case scenario.

With all 72 roof trusses unloaded in the street, Tim and I immediately started cutting the ties that held the trusses together from their transportation and carried them one by one from the road to the job-site where the house was being built.

Back and forth, trip after trip, Tim and I carried the trusses as fast as we could, reassuring all of the spectating neighbors who were still blocked in their driveways that we were trying to resolve the issue as quickly as possible. Keeping in mind that each truss can weigh up to a few hundred pounds, each one specifically engineered for an exact location on the roof, we had to be extremely cognizant of where we were placing them.

This event took place so early in the morning that the framing crew – who were still arriving at the job-site – hardly had a chance to absorb the magnitude of the situation. Yet, despite their tired eyes and looks of disbelief, they immediately jumped into action assisting Tim and me. Quickly and effectively as a team, we were able to redistribute the lumber safely from off of the middle of the street and onto the construction site. We knew the neighbors would be blocked-in for hours or nearly an entire day if we waited on equipment. In this type of situation, the framers normally would have never agreed to move roof trusses by hand due to the difficulty and demands of their labor-intensive requirements within their normal day. They would have asked us to rent a forklift or similar equipment for them to move the trusses. But we knew that if the crew saw their managers willing to do whatever it took in this unfortunate situation, they would join us without hesitation.

    Tim and I decided to take that proactive step to begin unloading the trusses ourselves knowing it would work out in our favor. That was the moment, under the demanding pressure and quick decision-making, when I truly began to obtain a significant understanding of what it means to be adaptable, and how crucial it is to be critically aware of what's happening in my environment.

Amongst the knowledge and experience that I gained daily, was a profound sense of resilience. I no longer felt like an outcast or bystander as the only woman present on the job-site. Because I had taken action to solve an issue no one had control over, I was fully seen and recognized as a suitable and adaptable leader who was willing to learn and tackle the hard stuff. I was accepted by everyone as an individual who is capable of stepping up and stepping in, and I was grateful for both the opportunities and challenges that allowed me to do so. With this feeling of acceptance, I began to feel an intrinsic desire to dismantle the stereotypes regarding women in construction. I wanted to prove that I could do what needed to be done despite being a female and new to the home-building process. And what better place to start than with a worst-case scenario? I was presented with an opportunity. This opportunity to step up and step in grew and transformed me exponentially, and I became determined not to take that for granted.

LEARNING TO ADAPT

It is a commonly known fact that every human at their core possesses some ability to adapt. I believe that expanding our adaptability skills in conjunction with our critical awareness skills can be a key feature of learning to accept change as it comes our way. When incorporating these two skills into our lives, they can become a significant aid in overcoming obstacles during difficult circumstances and ultimately lead to success.

Creativity and flexibility are a must when faced with these types of situations. Not just for an ideal outcome, but more importantly for your own sanity. It is essential to recognize when to fight battles and when to bend and mold to the situation so that it benefits everyone involved. When you possess critical awareness skills, you and your team proactively adapt and pivot as soon as things start to go south. The benefits of adapting can minimize stress and potentially eliminate disorganization and hesitation from others during the process.

Individuals are best set up to succeed in challenging work environments when they improve their ability to be adaptable. Without the willingness to adapt to their surroundings, a person can crumble under the stress causing their hard work and their relationships with coworkers and management to suffer. Adaptability allows an individual to have a sense of internal balance and flexibility, which in turn gives them the ability to respond positively to stressful situations.

One thing I found helpful was getting into the habit of doing a thorough mental assessment of my environment daily. This included writing down key information after the mental assessment was complete. This tactic helped to lessen the blow of any problem that arose so that I could naturally become more prepared to adapt and accept the change. Accepting complications and constant changes now became part of the adaptation process, and needless to say, my skills of becoming highly adaptive to my environment amplified, since no single day on the job-site is the same as the previous day. It is hard to accept that plans and agendas do not often pan out as expected. Standing by and being ready to adapt as necessary minimizes stress when those plans inevitably change.

    We have all experienced successes and failures at some point in our lives and will continue to experience them, but I was in no way accustomed to experiencing such constant large-scale failures as the construction environment had in store for me. Before learning the importance of adapting, I easily became disheartened, confused, or highly stressed showing up to the construction site every morning only to learn about some type of issue whether it be in, or oftentimes out of my control.

On a regular basis, it was no easy feat dealing with a last-minute discovery that vital material was either missing, damaged, had gotten lost during the delivery process, or the wrong type of material was delivered. There were often recurring time-sensitive scenarios where drivers would get stuck – due to poor weather conditions – and unable to deliver large pieces of lumber. Coming across a delay like that would lead to a pile of scheduling backups for myself and others. Adapting for me meant that I was free to choose the least difficult option which often included last-minute decisions of unloading the lumber myself in order to prevent a scheduling nightmare or building delay.

Speaking of the effort involved when it comes to adapting, I'll never forget the day I discovered that our building materials had been stuck (for days at this point and with no end in sight) on a boat halfway across the world in the Suez Canal, Egypt. My biggest complication was that this material was scheduled to be installed within a few days by a subcontractor who was booked out for months with appointments. On top of that, there were no other subcontractors available for this type of work until the following year! This meant that if I hadn't changed plans and scrambled to get customer approval for new material that could arrive within the allotted time frame for installation, this impact would have derailed our entire completion deadline causing a financial burden to both my company and the customer.

This was just one of the scenarios where I had to learn to adapt and adapt fast, even if I didn't have all the answers. It's easy to let the stress of a situation cloud your thinking at the moment of decision. One key that enabled me to continue managing well was learning to accept the uncomfortable facts of a situation. Then, pause just long enough to emerge from the frustration and creatively find a way to keep things moving, whether it meant completely changing directions or revamping a methodology. I operated out of the understanding that making a decision under frustration while in the grips of high stress would only cloud my mind and prevent my ability to think clearly and cohesively.

Since I had to often rely on the team around me, I also had to gain the self-confidence that I could find a way to figure it out. That approach alone is what aided my ability to not let my frustration overwhelm my creative thinking capacity.

GAINING A SENSE OF BELONGING

When faced with adversity in an unknown situation or a new environment, having a plan is important. However, having the ability to deviate from that plan is vital for achievement. I believe that having this ability becomes an easier task when a person feels supported or connected to their environment. When we feel connected to an environment, it brings forth an ability to cope with difficult situations more effectively, therefore – allowing resilience to be cultivated and practiced.

Imagine with me for a moment that you're trying to produce work in an environment where you don't feel like you belong, which can be fairly normal. At the same time, I want you to picture feeling some form of anxiety or fear or displacement from that environment and your surroundings, as they are all new to you. It would seem difficult to be productive day in and day out and produce quality work, would it not?

With this level of fear and detachment present, fundamental imagination and creativity are stunted. Stress can be high, productivity is exceptionally low, and the fear of failing is great. Now imagine you are working in an environment where you feel you belong and are fully supported – your failures and lack of knowledge are accepted as opportunities for growth. Can you imagine the possibilities? As a leader, I wanted to exemplify promoting this feeling of belonging and worth in the workplace.

I eventually found myself wanting to belong to the construction environment, despite how uncomfortable it felt at first.

Once I gained that sense of belonging, I then found myself becoming more resilient against a changing and disruptive environment. That allowed me to think more clearly under stress and make more efficient decisions. When we feel connected to our environment, we are more inclined to be relaxed. When we are relaxed, we are more likely to come up with innovative solutions to problems. This is especially helpful when the environment in which we're working can be unpredictable.

    I truly believe in the importance of finding a sense of belonging to your environment, because without it, it becomes nearly impossible to thrive or succeed. As you begin to find a sense of belonging, you create the ability to increase your understanding and awareness of that environment as well as be able to accept it for what it is. This environmental acceptance provides you with a compelling reason to lean into the discomfort that you were once surrounded by. And as you would guess, when we decide to lean into discomfort (or confront fear) this naturally provokes growth within us and brings forth confidence about our abilities that we may not have had.

    I am choosing to share my personal experience of this life-changing event because I see how so much headache, stress, and insurmountable pressure could have been avoided if I had possessed the ability to accept the environment as it was. I know many people struggle with accepting their circumstances and allowing themselves to be okay with belonging to something new and something so vastly different than they have ever known. I will never claim to have all the answers for how to best adjust to change. But learning how to effectively plan for potential and future issues in the workplace is something everyone can agree is of paramount importance. And without obtaining critical thinking abilities, this anticipation will never take place.

If anyone were to ask me after fifteen years of personal and group training, if I could effectively manage multiple custom home-building sites at once, including the organizing and logistical work of more than one hundred people, I would have laughed at the thought. I had no qualifications for construction. Looking back, the only reason why I survived the career change at all was due in large part to my adaptability. Had I not been willing to exercise my skills of adaptability, my time in the field would have been a short-lived disaster. I found myself face-to-face with countless intimidating situations every day. And every day I began to see those as new opportunities for personal learning and growth and a way to develop my skills of resilience to my environment.

Chapter Four Takeaways

- Trust in your abilities to adapt while you're learning.

- Taking on challenges can help increase your resilience.

- The more you focus on what you can control, the less stressed you'll be about what you can't control.

- Take a moment to breathe. Acting too quickly out of frustration will only cloud your decision process.

- Always prepare for the unexpected.

- You are free to fail as long as you accept those failures as opportunities for growth.

- When you fail to prepare, you prepare to fail.
  - Benjamin Franklin

Chapter Five

The Power of Community

Do not let what you cannot do interfere with what you can do.

- John Wooden

My risk was high. Within a small company, a leader's failure is everyone's failure. The pressure to deliver a quality home within a reasonable timeframe, during a global pandemic, rested on my shoulders. A lot of people were relying on me to succeed and move seamlessly from one project to the next. It was my job to manage the construction flow and logistics while maintaining a steady working system throughout. I know for certain that a good outcome would have been nearly impossible to achieve if it wasn't for the teamwork attributes demonstrated by everyone involved.

Although I was under a large amount of pressure at the time, this adversity helped affirm my confidence that I could accomplish what I set out to do. When the goal is for everyone involved in a project to succeed, no matter the odds, the team dynamics improve significantly.

In this chapter, I want to highlight the importance of strong teamwork across an organization. The success of the entire group depends on the success of each individual member of the group. If one person fails, the whole group fails. After all, if you are only as strong as your weakest link, team synergy is all-important. I wanted to be someone who could set an example as a leader and I knew that would require me to fully gain the alliance of the subcontractors in order to succeed, especially while I was learning a new field.

COLLABORATION

The teamwork and community that was built around and within the job-site became essential to the development and completion of projects that otherwise would have ceased operation. I figured out very quickly that you cannot buy time, trust, or loyalty; you must earn these. So, that is what I set out to do. My success and that of my company depended on it. These components of teamwork and the knowledge of building solid community support were the strongest assets I had in a field completely new to me. The challenges I faced would have been much more significant without the help of a good team.

I firmly believe that the collaboration of individuals in support of an end goal (or something greater than themselves), is one of the significant components of feeling a sense of purpose and belonging within any new or challenging environment. This type of togetherness attitude and conscious collaboration offers an equal opportunity for each person to gain trust for, and from one another. Trust builds connection, and in my opinion, in order for someone to be successful at anything, they need to build trust and make connections with those around them.

In correlation to my situation, I strongly relate to what long-time Duke basketball head coach, Mike Krzyzewski said about trust and team building: "If you set up an atmosphere of communication and trust, it becomes tradition. Older team members will establish your credibility with newer ones. Even if they don't like everything about you, they'll still say, 'He's (she's) trustworthy, committed to us as a team." I am grateful to have had many examples of this play out in real-life experiences, all of which were due to the reputation that Tim already carried amongst the subcontractors.

There was one particular instance that took me by surprise. It just so happened to be during the middle of summer, in the height of the afternoon heat. Everyone was tired and moving slower than usual. I had just finished working in the crawl space of the home to prepare for our final inspection while I awaited our appliances to be delivered. The siding crew was also on-site and was finishing up the exterior of the home. At the time the appliances were delivered, an issue arose with the driver and his equipment. This unfortunately resulted in the driver leaving the brand new oven range, microwave, and dishwasher, still in their boxes near the street, over one hundred yards away from the actual house. The driver was so far behind on deliveries that he no sooner left than he arrived, leaving me stranded on the street with the appliances and out of options or ideas of how to get them inside.

Not much longer after I managed to bring the microwave inside and the dishwasher closer to the house, the siding crew took notice. They quickly dismounted from their ladders and rushed to assist me without any questions or hesitations. They, of course, were just as confused as I was as to how someone would leave their product and me, in that type of situation. Nonetheless, they understood that it would require a team of people, which I did not have available, to move the massive boxes safely inside the home.

THE POWER OF COMMUNITY

It can be fair to assume that the majority of people prefer to experience some sort of balanced connection within their work environment. (If you prefer chaos more power to you – you're in the minority.) But having a powerful sense of connection allows an individual to operate at a much higher level than if they felt little connection to those around them. A connection can also act as a driving force to continue moving forward during times of difficulty. After my co-worker's car accident and stroke, I was astounded at how quickly the construction community came together to support me in my new role.

This support made an extraordinary impact on how I began to successfully operate as a manager and leader. It was the backing of this team and community that ultimately led to my success. I feel it's important to mention that so much of my workload and the impact I created wouldn't have been nearly as possible if it wasn't for the hardworking and dedicated men that I worked alongside day in and day out. I had to learn very quickly how to relinquish my own control over a situation and trust in each one of their abilities as they stepped up to accept such an immense task during the time of my co-workers' absence.

    One example of this incredible support came from a subcontractor from whom I would have least expected it. This subcontractor was our carpenter. He was a younger guy running his own company, and like everyone building or remodeling during the early pandemic, he was also backed up for weeks on end with work.

    It was the day after Tim's accident. I was still comprehending how I was going to accomplish everything by myself since the timing of his return to work was unknown, if he would be able to come back at all. With over one hundred subcontractors who still had no idea of the circumstance, I began the process of informing them one by one that I was now the sole person responsible until further notice. Late that same evening, I was feeling heavy and still shaken with disbelief that I was in this situation. I was trying not to drown in the storm of emotions that I felt. When I finally called my carpenter, he immediately sensed how fearful and distressed I was.

He was also good friends with Tim, so he already knew the pressure I was feeling. He understood that my co-worker's role was vital to our operation as a small business. And despite his worries and schedule restraints, he was quick to reassure me that he would support me no matter what would come next. What surprised me most is that he immediately placed his confidence in me and didn't hesitate to offer whatever help I needed. He acknowledged the complexity of the situation, and without missing a beat we worked together as a team to make adjustments and arrangements as necessary. But, because I had previously devoted time and energy to building trust and connection with my carpenter and his crew, they in turn were quick to trust me without question. We all came closer together as a group and as a result of the conscious effort placed on *the importance of teamwork and collaboration.* This type of collaboration continued to fuel my desire even more to build connections with all of the people working around me.

Another significant example demonstrating the power of community was a phone call I had that same evening with the representative of our building material supplier, Jeff. Jeff had known Tim for most of his life and he knew what a hard and honest worker Tim was. Jeff also knew that as a small company, we had enough work on our plate similar to that of a larger, nationally known builder. It was a rare occasion for one person to be in charge of that amount of work, and needless to say, Jeff found himself in as much shock as I was about the situation.

Neither Jeff nor I could believe that something like this happened. It seemed like a nightmare. We were all still in disbelief and at this point, no one knew if Tim would be able to walk again.

The realness of the situation began to set in even more than the previous day. As I held back tears of discouragement and fear about the unknown challenges ahead, Jeff continued to speak calmly. Included in his list of encouragements to me were comments like:

"We will do whatever we can to help you."

"You're not in this alone, I can promise you that."

"I know it can be tough and confusing out there, but you'll get the hang of it."

Jeff works with one of the biggest national building suppliers in the nation and was a representative of about 25 builders in my area. I figured I was just another fish in the sea to him, but I began to realize something as our conversation continued. Jeff and Tim had a powerful connection that went beyond Tim just being another cog in a machine. Jeff cared personally about Tim, which also meant he cared personally about me, and that realization put me at ease. I was beginning to more fully understand the importance of growing and maintaining strong relationships within the construction community I was now a part of, and how beneficial they can be.

IT TAKES A VILLAGE

Those seemingly small but significant conversations drove home to me the value of the connections that I was attempting to build in the construction industry – relationships of trust, respect, and integrity. I felt it would be crucial to collect those relationships for a rainy day moment of crisis down the road, just like the one I was experiencing. It made me realize that maybe I wasn't as alone and isolated as I first thought when I entered construction. I found that when you establish a connection and credibility with those around you, you're guaranteeing that credibility to be projected onto those succeeding you, at first. Then, it becomes up to them to build on and keep that credibility.

That realization sparked another one for me: if I could do that in the construction world – accomplish what few others thought possible – then I knew for certain other women could do it too. That was an impact I felt like I could be proud of and I focused my efforts on working hard to achieve that goal. My ability to do what seemed unfathomable during a moment of crisis came as a direct result of who I was surrounded by and the effort put into developing those relationships. I am walking proof that no one achieves nearly what they are capable of alone, as when they work with a team of others.

When it was all said and done, what I found most encouraging during that chaotic time in the industry was remembering to take a step back to realize that we are all facing similar difficulties in life, and within each of our own respective environments, our responses (rather than reactions) to those situations can make a world of difference.

Through this experience, I came to realize that what I was striving for was to be an example to a larger audience than my work team – to empower other women and show them that they have the potential to step up and step out from the comfort of their current situation and pursue something that they have never given a second thought to. Whether the delay is due to existing fears or assumptions that they have no space in a particular industry, that is all changing in our world today.

I am here to assure you that no matter the current adversity you may be facing, you are not alone. Sometimes it can be difficult to convince yourself that if you take the risk and leap into the unknown, that it will be worth it.

But, I believe that taking a calculated risk to pursue something so different can become truly eye-opening and satisfying.

NOTES

1. "Women in Construction: The State of the Industry in 2022," BigRentz, January 6, 2022, https://www.bigrentz.com/blog/women-construction#:~:text=There%20are%20several%20factors%20that,their%20path%20in%20the%20industry.

2. Sundiatu Dixon-Fyle, Kevin Dolan, Dame Vivian Hunt and Sara Prince. "Diversity wins: How inclusion matters." May 19, 2020.

   https://www.mckinsey.com/featured-insights/diversity-and-inclusion/diversity-wins-how-inclusion-matters.

3. Hernán Cortés. In *Wikipedia.* Last modified December 6, 2022. https://en.wikipedia.org/wiki/Hern%C3%A1n_Cort%C3%A9s.

4. "APA Dictionary of Psychology," American Psychology Association, assessed March 10, 2022.

   https://dictionary.apa.org/resilience.

5. "Statistics of Women in Construction." The National Association of Women in Construction, assessed April 4, 2022.

   https://www.nawic.org/statistics.

www.ingramcontent.com/pod-product-compliance
Lightning Source LLC
Chambersburg PA
CBHW072144170526
45158CB00004BA/1496